Self-Discipline

Mental Toughness

A Guide to Developing Your Grit and Increasing Your Productivity

Table of Contents

Introduction

Congratulations on downloading your personal copy of *Self-Discipline and Mental Toughness: A Guide to Developing Your Grit and Increasing Your Productivity*. Thank you for doing so.

Self-discipline is a useful, important life skill necessary for successful people. Regardless of the area of life you're setting goals in, this skill will be essential. Although most people already know that it's important, there aren't many who actually take proactive steps to build and strengthen it in themselves.

The Misconception About Self-Discipline

There's a common belief about self-discipline being restrictive, tough, harsh, or limiting, but this is far from true. Self-discipline is about inner strength, knowing yourself, and having control. This valuable trait will allow you to follow through on your decisions, stick to your path, and accomplish amazing feats in life.

What Can This Trait Give You?

You will overcome laziness and procrastination, beat addictions, and radiate a strong sense of will. This book will give you the tools you need to build up a powerful sense of self-discipline, the fuel for your greatest desires. As you can see, you have nothing to lose other than some bad habits. So, if you're ready to change your life for the better, let's get to it. Thank you for choosing this book!

Chapter 1: Success, Motivation, and Choices

Success is something all of us crave, whether it's an ideal of how we want to look, how much money we'll earn, or even the type of family we'll eventually have. The idea of success almost seems, to many of us, like an elusive secret. We glorify the concept, place those who have success on a pedestal, and separate ourselves from it. But the truth is, success isn't a secret. If this is true, what is success? It's a *process*.

The Success Process

Success is not something you suddenly achieve one day; it's an attitude, a way of thinking, and a path to living. The subject that you want to gain self-discipline in will be highly personal for you, but there are some general guidelines that can help you along the way. How can you begin the process of success?

- **Define What Success Means to You:** Take some time to really think about this. What is the most important thing in the world to you? Who do you want to reach with your message? What does the ultimate vision of success look like for you? How will you know when you've gotten there? As soon as you have defined success for yourself, you'll be able to get on the path towards it.

- **Know Your Vision is Possible:** You won't be able to work towards your goal if you don't already believe in your heart it can happen for you. Once you've figured out what you desire, seek out other people who have already achieved this goal (either in person, in books, or online). This will inspire you and give you proof that your goal is possible!

- **Act No Matter What:** If you're going to wait around for the perfect time to act, you'll be waiting forever. You cannot depend on always feeling motivated to do something, even when it's something you deeply care about. Force yourself to take action, even on days that you're feeling lazy, and it will seriously pay off.

- **Try to Help Others:** Humans are social beings. We need connection. Providing and giving value to those around you will help you build stronger social ties that you can fall back on during hard times. Helping other people can also inspire us to stay on our personal path toward success. Instead of asking what you can get from any social interaction you're having, ask yourself what you can give. Success is not something selfish, but something only meaningful when it's shared.

The Truth About Motivation

How does motivation work? Oftentimes, this word brings thoughts of bonuses at work, material gains, or extra vacation. But the reality is, motivation is something more elusive than that. It's highly personal and, at times, not even reliable.

Deep, Intrinsic Motivation

If you aren't truly motivated to do a task, intrinsically (meaning you love doing it for its own sake), you probably won't do it. If you're only motivated by external awards, you likely won't stick to your goal.

Take the example of wanting to lose weight. Telling yourself you'll look much better may work for the first week in terms of getting you to the gym, but eventually, you will probably stop going. Reminding yourself that you want a longer life and that you deserve to feel great from the inside out, on the other hand, can be an intrinsic, meaningful source of motivation.

When and Why Motivation Doesn't Work

Sometimes, motivation just isn't effective. No matter how good our intentions are, all it takes is a different mood to slip up on our goals. Motivation can be a fleeting, changing state. This is why you can set your alarm at night, feeling motivated to arise at 6 in the morning and have a super productive day, only to groan and hit snooze when it goes off. For this reason, self-discipline is a far more reliable system than motivation.

<u>You Have a Choice in Life</u>

We have all been around people who seem to lose their minds when something stressful happens, completely shutting down and giving up. They act as though their states of being are out of their control, essentially forfeiting their own choice in the matter. But the truth is that though we can't always control stressful events in life, we can control how we react to them.

An event outside of you can only cause you to stress out if you make the choice to do so. I understand that when you're in the midst of a chaotic situation, your reaction feels like anything but a choice. But the fact is that stress is something we all go through in life. What differs is how we handle it and the best way to control how we handle it is through self-discipline. If you don't have a strong enough desire to learn how to handle stress in the right way, you won't do it. It's a decision.

Stress is constantly around us, but it doesn't become a part of you until you accept and internalize it. Everyone engages in stressed-out behavior every so often, but it doesn't have to be a habit. Here are the steps to control your reactions:

- **Notice them:** When an event pops up that makes you veer off course (whether it's giving up on your goal of losing weight and deciding to eat donuts or procrastinating on that test you're supposed to be studying for), notice it. What are the triggers that throw you off?

- **Record them:** The next step will be to write these triggers down along with the results that came from them. Now, these may not be nice to look at, but a truly self-disciplined person isn't afraid to view their faults. Only when you know what they are can you control and improve them.

- **Tiny Steps:** Now that you're fully aware of your weaknesses, it's time to make small changes toward shifting them. If you know, for example, that walking through the mall and smelling popcorn triggers you to want to give up on your healthy eating plan, stay away from the mall. If you tend to get angry whenever a certain relative calls, do some deep breathing exercises before you talk to them. These small shifts end up leading to big changes over time.

Chapter 2: Your Purpose and Positivity

Most people have no idea what they would like to do with their life. Some assume that it will eventually become clear to them as they get older, once they complete school, or once they're married. But the truth is that you may still have no clue, even after going through these big changes. Part of the difficulty with this question is the idea of "purpose" in life.

Many of us have a ton of baggage attached to this idea. We may believe that it's such a huge deal, or that without it, we're doomed to live a life of misery. Needless to say, this puts a bit too much pressure on the quest to find our life purpose. Try to approach the situation with a fresh perspective and an attitude of curiosity.

Questions for Finding Your Purpose

Finding your purpose should be an interesting, fun process and not something you dread or feel is an obligation. Feel free to mix and match these questions, or even add some of your own.

1. What Would You Do if Money Were No Object?

How would you spend your life if you already had all of your financial concerns covered? Perhaps you'd spend your days painting, helping other people through volunteer work, or golfing with your friends. Whatever this passion is, it's time to dedicate more of your life to it. It may become your life purpose, or it may just give you an outlet for relaxation and happiness. Either way is conducive to finding out what your purpose in life is.

2. Can You Handle Sacrifice for Your Dream?

The fact is that everything worthwhile in life involves sacrifice and comes at a cost. How much sacrifice can you deal with to reach your goal? Knowing the answer to this question will allow you to figure out how realistic one pursuit is in comparison with another. Here are some examples of sacrifices you may have to deal with if you pursue a specific path:

- If you want to be an entrepreneur, are you ready to face rejection time and time again?

- Do you want to be a writer without ever facing critique?

- Are you ready to give hours and hours of your day to your interest?

If these negative potential outcomes are enough to turn you away from something, then the goal is not your true path.

3. What Did You Love as a Child?

Certain things never change in a person. Oftentimes, what your favorite pastime was as a child can tell you a lot about what your life purpose could be now. For instance, maybe you loved to write stories as a kid and spent days doing it for the sheer joy and immersion it brought you. Odds are, whatever this interest was for you as a kid, you don't do nearly as much anymore. This could be because we've become self-conscious about our interest or that we only think things are worthwhile if they bring financial gain.

One of your first steps for reconnecting with your life purpose should be revisiting whatever it was your childhood self loved to spend hours doing. As a kid, do you think you would have stopped doing something just because you didn't think it was profitable or good enough? No, you would have done what you loved just because you loved it. Reconnect with that part of you.

4. When Do You Forget Time Exists?

Everyone has had an experience of the flow state, that state of mind that is so immersive that you forget to eat dinner. Maybe you get so immersed in coding that you don't leave your apartment for an entire day, which could be a big clue as to what your life purpose could be. Even an activity that is not typically thought of as "productive" such as gaming, could give you a hint as to what's important to you.

- **The Qualities Behind the Activity:** Taking the example of gaming, if you spend all day immersed in this activity, it could point to several traits or interests in you. You could thrive on a competitive atmosphere, for goal-setting, or general improvement in life conditions.

- **Applying those Qualities:** When you can apply the obsession you feel for self-competition and improvement to your passion or business, this will take you very far. For you, this could mean efficient organization, teaching, fixing problems, or something related to your social life. Whatever the case, make sure you are looking at the principles behind the activities to find what it is that makes it so

addictive and compelling to you. These
principles can be applied in other areas, too.

5. Being Okay with Vulnerability

When you're new to something, or rather
inexperienced, you are probably going to be clueless at
first. That's just the way it goes. And to be bad at
something means you might end up embarrassing
yourself and feeling vulnerable, probably over and
over again. It's completely normal for people to try to
avoid embarrassment, because it doesn't feel very
good. But if everyone were to avoid the potential of
doing something embarrassing, they would never
reach new heights!

- **Acceptance:** You have to teach yourself to be
  okay with being vulnerable. At this moment,

there's probably something you'd love to be learning about or pursuing, but reasons behind why you don't. These reasons are likely something you repeat to yourself on a regular basis. Often, these reasons have to do with potential reactions of other people to what you might do. Do you worry about being judged by your peers if you fail? Do you worry about your parents not accepting your new path? Then you're focusing on the wrong factors.

Accepting the possibility that others may not agree with your path and that it matters enough to you to stick with is the key here. Everything great on this planet is unconventional, unique, and to some people, shocking. So, you have to go against what others think to do anything amazing. This can be very frightening due to the fear of looking foolish or getting embarrassed. But what is the price to pay for ignoring your inner calling? Is it worth it to suppress yourself just to avoid a bit of embarrassment or scorn?

- **Seeing Your Newbie Status as a Strength:** A lot of times, experts or people who are very experienced in a certain field get stuck in concepts and don't know where to go. They find it hard to think creatively. For this reason, being new to something can actually be an advantage. You're seeing everything in the field with new eyes. This can apply to anything from business, to playing an instrument, to general self-improvement tasks. Someone who has a fresh, blank perspective can often see connections where others struggle.

6. Find Out How You Can Help

As I mentioned before, we are social beings and helping each other is important. Unless you live under a rock, you already know that the world has no shortage of current problems to focus on. What speaks most to you in this sea of issues? In order to be happy and satisfied in life, it's important to be a part of something bigger that benefits others. Here are some ideas for getting involved:

- **Helping the Homeless:** Do you feel a tug on your heartstrings any time you see a homeless person on the street? Don't ignore this! That could mean that you would get a lot out of volunteering your time at a shelter or finding other ways to help your fellow humans in need.

- **Writing about Issues:** Our education system isn't very great, domestic violence is a problem, and mental healthcare could use some improvement. All of these are issues you could be helping to spread the word about. Do you have a blog or a writing talent? Start using it to get information about something you care about.

Find something to care about and put your energies into helping. This won't mean you'll fix the issue on your own, but you will feel that you've made a difference, however small. And feeling connected to something and knowing you're making small, positive changes can do wonders for your self-esteem and will likely get you a little closer to finding your true purpose in life.

7. What Do You Want to be Remembered For?

Imagine that you just got a cancer diagnosis and know that you'll die within half a year. Yes, I know, it's not fun to think about dying and can be a scary thought. But this can give you many practical benefits. One of them is that it helps you discern what matters most to you in your life from what is pure, useless distraction. A lot of people wouldn't know how to answer this question, so if you have a little difficulty thinking of something on the spot, don't worry. Give it some thought before you find the answer. Here are other related questions to ponder:

- **What Will You Leave Behind?** How will

  others remember you once you leave this

  earth? Will it be mostly positive things or

  negative things? What can you do to make sure

  that you're remembered in a positive light

  when you leave this earth? If you can't think of

  anything but people saying impressive stuff

  about what you owned when you were alive,

  you probably aren't digging deep enough.

- **What are Your Values?** If you're having

  trouble deciding how you want people to

  remember you, it could be that you aren't sure

  what your values are or what matters most to

  you in life. This leaves you open to the danger

  of taking on the priorities of other people and

  allowing them to direct your life instead of you.

  This path can never lead to true happiness or

fulfilling relationships.

- **The Writing Test:** If you *still* don't know what your values or purpose are, it's time to do the writing test to get a little deeper. Get a piece of paper (or an empty text document on your computer, though actually writing with a pen feels more personal) and write at the top "What am I on this earth for?" Does this sound dramatic? Good! Now just start writing. At first, you may find that it's hard to know what to say but keep going. Keep digging and questioning until the words start flowing naturally. This should give you some clarity.

Figuring out what your purpose is means finding out what cause or goal you can be a part of that is larger than you or the people around you. It's not about earning $50,000 more per year or finally dating that specific person; it's bigger than that. How would your time be best spent? How can you make it more meaningful? If nothing comes to mind, you need to get out there and experiment more to find it. And that brings me to something else that will help you immensely along the way...

The Power of Positivity

Positive thinking is a bit of a buzzword these days, but what does it really mean? Although it's a no-brainer that most of us want to be more positive than negative, it's also a term that is so widely used it's lost a bit of its original meaning. But research is starting to reveal that it's about more than being upbeat and in a good, happy mood. Positive thinking can bring true value to your life, strengthen your self-discipline, and lead to all sorts of other useful skills in work and your personal life.

The results that positive thinking can have on your professional life, relationships, and even health is currently being observed by experts in psychology. Frederickson, a researcher of positive psychology at North Carolina university has found a few surprising new facts about how positive thinking can impact your skills in life. These useful bits of information can be applied practically to your life and self-discipline goals, no matter what they are specifically focused on. Here are some ideas from her research.

The Impact of Negativity

Science has known for a while that negative feelings prompt the brain to perform something specific.

When you encounter a potentially life-threatening situation, you get out of there as fast as you can. Suddenly, nothing else in your surroundings matters whatsoever in comparison. You will be focused completely on the threat, the state of mind created by the threat, and how to save yourself. Even if you do have a wide variety of choices available to you in the moment, your mind will narrow its focus and hone in on only one.

- **How This Developed:** In the early days of human development, this is a trait that saved our skins countless times, no doubt. Encountering a wild predator is one example of a scenario where that particular brain function would have come in handy. However, this is the modern world and that tendency can get in the way a lot of the time, rather than help us. Our brains are programmed to feel a threat (however insignificant in actuality) and turn the world off, limiting options and creating tunnel vision.

- **Examples of Negativity Tunnel Vision:** Imagine that you just got into an argument with your best friend and had to go to work immediately after. Odds are, in this situation, you would have a very hard time focusing on work and instead would be replaying the scenario over and over in your mind. Or what about those days where you know you have a task list a foot long and can't seem to prompt yourself to get started on any of the items on the list? In each scenario, your negative thoughts are closing you off to thinking creatively or seeing other choices.

The Impacts of Positivity

Now it's time to compare this with what happens in your brain when you are having positive thoughts.

- **The Experiment:** Fredrickson looked at the way positive emotions impacted the brain in an experiment where subjects were divided into groups and shown various video clips. The first group was shown images that prompted joyful feelings, while the second group looked at clips that made them feel content. A third group was the "neutral" group that was shown clips that had no emotion attached to them. Finally, there were two more groups shown feelings of fear and anger, respectively.

- **The Results:** After the groups were shown these clips, all of the participants were asked to envision a scenario that would prompt similar feelings and to record on a piece of paper how they would react. Each of them were given a sheet of paper with 20 sentences that began with "I would like to..." The group members that viewed images related to anger and fear recorded fewer responses. The group members who viewed content and joyful images listed many more actions they wanted to take compared to both the negative groups and the neutral group.

- **What Does This Show?** This experiment showed that when someone is feeling love, contentment, and joyful feelings, they will have more ideas and see more options. These were some of the first scientific findings that showed that positive thinking can broaden possibilities and have a mind-opening impact. But that's not all...

Positive Thinking and Other Skills

Positive thinking leads to even more advantages than great feelings and more possibilities. Actually, the greatest advantage that positive thinking brings is a stronger ability to develop resources and build skills that will help you later on in your life.

- **Unexpected Advantages:** Enjoyable habits can bring unexpected benefits. For instance, a kid who spends a lot of time outside with his friends, climbing trees, builds up the skills of athletic movement, social communication, and

creative reasoning. In this example, the
positive feelings of joy and play help the child
to develop skills that will help them in other
areas of life later on. And these traits end up
lasting a lot longer than the positive feelings
that prompted them in the first place.

- **A Solid Foundation:** Later in the future, the
  positive foundation of social skills could lead to
  a prosperous career in team management. The
  joy that brought about the creation and
  exploration of new traits isn't there anymore,
  while the lasting impacts are. Positive feelings
  open you up to new possibilities, bringing you
  brand new resources and skills and giving more
  value to unrelated and often unexpected areas
  in life. This is the opposite of what negative
  feelings do. So, the next question is, how can

you be more positive in life to get these great benefits?

How to Think More Positively

What actionable steps can you take to improve your skill of positive thinking? To start with, any action or activity that brings you feelings of love, contentment, or joy can help with this. You likely already have a few ideas in mind for that. It could be playing piano, hanging out with your spouse, or cooking. Here are some other general tasks to focus on that will bring you more positive emotions and benefits:

- **Positive Journaling:** Do you keep a journal? If not, it's time to start. Not only will this help you develop self-discipline by ensuring you stick with your goal of writing each day, but it can help you become more positive. In one study, a group of 90 participants were split into two different groups. One group was asked to write each day, for three days, on something intensely positive. The other group wrote on a neutral topic. A few months later, the participants who did positive journaling for three days had to visit the doctor less frequently and reported better moods and fewer sicknesses.

- **Make Time for Play:** Make some time in your life for playing. The average person schedules appointments, events, and meetings, so why not pencil in some playtime for yourself? Have you ever set aside an hour just for experimentation and exploration? Do you ever carve out some time specifically for fun and enjoyment? Happiness is at least as important as that work conference you have on your calendar, yet a lot of people don't act like this is true. Make time for this in your life and you will reap the wonderful benefits of positivity.

- **Gratitude Lists:** Looking for things to be grateful for is another great way to increase the amount of positivity present in your life. This can be done first thing in the morning or right before going to sleep (or if you really want to go above and beyond, both!) and can be done mentally or on paper. Make a list of what you are grateful for in that moment, no matter how seemingly small or big. Even if it's something like "The sun is shining today," that's a good start.

The Illusion of Putting Off Happiness

Most of us believe that success is what leads to happiness. And it's true that certain situations can bring you more joy. But having this perspective as a default might be preventing you from experiencing more happiness in your life. Do you often think that as soon as you make a specific change in your life you will finally be happy? Or maybe you think that once you buy a certain item, you'll feel joy again. How often does it actually happen? Chances are, you feel great for a short while and then it fades.

All of us are guilty of doing this to some degree. But the research on positivity we just covered should be enough to show you that happiness can be a great precursor for building the habits that will lead to success. So, happiness is not always the result of what you achieve but can also be the reason for your success. Happy people build new skills, gain new successes because of them, then feel even more joy, repeating this upward spiral ad infinitum.

Start making time to feel more positive emotions in life, by playing a sport, doing something creative, or just spending more time with your loved ones. This will lower your stress levels, make you smile, and even improve your self-discipline. Positive emotions and creative exploration open the door for reflection and growth in your life. The key to sticking with your chosen path is self-discipline, and the burden will feel much lighter with a positive approach.

Chapter 3: Dealing with Failure and Increasing Productivity

When it comes to the subject of failure, our own pride can be our worst enemy. Once events in life begin going the wrong way, we might go into survival mode, trying to maintain composure and possibly even lying to ourselves. But these common reactions, like clinging to what's changing, or denial, can ruin our ability to grow and adapt to changes in our lives. It can be extremely difficult to admit it to ourselves when we've messed up and try to fix it. Or we might hastily scramble to fix things, only to make them worse through a lack of forethought or careful planning.

Another common reaction to personal failure or mistakes is to lie to ourselves, pretend they didn't happen, or act like the mistake was a far lesser deal than it really was. We might be so nervous about what happened that we miss out on a real opportunity to fix it. So, all of this begs the question, how can we successfully adapt to change and deal with failure with grace?

How to Adapt Successfully

In our complicated world, it's necessary to keep an experimental, adaptive mentality and approach in order to reach success. We also need this attitude to develop a strong sense of self-discipline and excel at our goals. It's impossible to predict ahead of time whether the ideas we have or the risks we take will pay off once we launch them. Oftentimes, failure is inevitable, but there's good news! There is a way to fail in a productive manner. Here are the guidelines for failing productively:

1. Mix It Up

When you put all your eggs in one basket, a single failure can be very devastating. For this reason, among others, it's good to mix it up. Just as you should diversify your investments to avoid big losses, you should also have a wide variety of interests and plans in terms of business or your personal life. Even when it comes to hobbies, constantly looking for fresh ideas will help you see that a failure in one area isn't the end of the world, and you'll always have something else to fall back on.

2. Be Honest with Yourself

The next step for dealing with failure with poise is being completely honest with yourself about it when it does occur. Mistakes become much worse when you dwell on them or constantly beat yourself up over what happened. In order to rise above this common reaction, it's crucial to learn to recognize when you have failed. One way to recognize failure is to constantly ask for feedback from your peers. Asking someone you trust how you're doing and for honest critique can help you see a bit more clearly.

3. Get Rid of Attachments

This is hard when you're dealing with matters that are important to you, but handling failure in the right way calls for maintaining a healthy sense of non-attachment to outcomes. This doesn't mean you won't care; it just means that a single loss won't completely devastate you and throw your life off track. Stay adaptable, look for ways to grow, and always have a plan B.

4. Ask What You Can Learn

The best way to handle failure with ease and get more out of it is to ask yourself what you can learn from what happened. You may consider a low sales month at your job a failure, but dwelling on that and telling yourself you're no good isn't going to help. Instead, ask yourself what you did differently that may have contributed to the streak of low sales. Then ask yourself what you can do to make it better. Construct an action plan and you're already on your way to being productive with your failures!

Mastering the Art of Self-Discipline

Any master gets amazing at their art or trade by consistent practice, an attitude of devotion, and an openness to learning more. This is the approach required to become a master of self-discipline. Here are some practices that will help you gain an unshakeable and reliable sense of discipline that you can always fall back on no matter what happens.

Do It, Even When You Don't Feel Like It

Procrastination is an issue that most of us are familiar with. We usually procrastinate by telling ourselves that we simply don't feel like doing the task right now. It could be that the task is intimidating, confusing, or difficult in some way and makes us feel uncomfortable. This could lead you to seek a distracting or pleasant activity to occupy yourself with instead. The amazing thing is, in this mentality, we can find endless ways to occupy ourselves that help us avoid the task we know we should be doing.

Before you can start trimming your nails, checking Facebook, or watering your plants to avoid the task, begin the task immediately. Right when your mind starts to chime in and try to convince you to do something else, just do it anyway. Oftentimes, the fear of the task itself is far worse than the action itself.

Start Exercising Every Day

This is one of the greatest ways to build self-discipline because it's something that nearly every one of us has put off in one way or another. Exercise can feel hard when you aren't used to it, so we distract ourselves with something else, putting it off until "tomorrow" every day. But this can be seen as an ordinary part of maintaining your health, like brushing your teeth and eating. Show up to your exercise even when you're tired or don't feel like it. Odds are, you won't ever feel perfectly ready to do it, but you'll never regret a completed workout.

Learn to Recognize Real Hunger

Most people get anxious when they're hungry and reach for the closest thing to eat, even if it's junk, but the truth is that a little hunger isn't bad for you. In fact, many times, we use our hunger as a distraction tactic to avoid doing what we should be doing. So next time you feel the urge to reach for a bag of potato chips, analyze your hunger and see if it's real or an excuse to distract yourself. This is just an exercise that will show you that it's possible to be more conscious about your automatic decisions. This could also help you lose weight if that's a goal you have.

Face the Issue

Most of us avoid thinking about problems in our lives.
Perhaps this is avoiding a financial problem, putting
off a big project, or ignoring the fact that you need to
get healthier. These realities can be hard to face
because again, they make us uncomfortable and we'd
rather ignore them. But try developing a new attitude
towards problems in your life. Next time you notice an
obstacle, see it as a different path. Acknowledge the
path, find out as much as you can about it, and learn
how to navigate. This will make you much stronger
and more disciplined as a person.

Be Direct in Conversation

Make it a goal to have uncomfortable conversations.
Most people avoid them because they can feel a little
awkward or scary. But doing this just leads to
problems including avoidance, resentment, and fights.

Instead of succumbing to the temptation of avoiding an awkward conversation at work or with your loved one, try to raise the issue in a compassionate, gentle and empathetic way. Ask them if you can talk, and then share your feelings. As long as you make sure you don't sound defensive and you do plenty of listening, it should go smoothly. Avoiding problems doesn't make them disappear, so get in the habit of facing your problems head on.

Look for the Good

Discipline is all about realizing that you don't need a huge, fancy award for everything you do. Getting things done is rewarding enough in itself. For example, you can learn how to relish going on a walk every morning instead of telling yourself that you can eat cake later if you do it. Or you can learn how to enjoy healthier foods instead of obsessively counting calories or dieting. Oftentimes, when you know how to look, the reward is in the new activity itself.

Remind Yourself of Intentions

One common challenge people undergo is staying true to their habit once the initial motivation wears off, as it inevitably does. It's not that hard to stick with something for a week, but it can get a little more challenging during the second or third week. Most people don't become masters of self-discipline because they quit before they get over the initial hump and don't give themselves enough time to establish momentum. Try committing to just one tiny habit for 60 days, even if it's only 5 to 10 minutes per day.

No matter what comes up, do this new activity each and every day at the same time and give yourself reminders on your phone or post-it notes around the house so you remember. Keep track of your progress on your calendar so you can see and celebrate your success. You can gradually add more and more positive, small habits. Before you know it, you will do these new habits without even giving them a second thought.

Using Self-Discipline to Become More Productive

There is no shortage of hacks, systems, articles, and tips on the internet that are designed to help with productivity and efficiency. But a lot of people who read blogs and books about productivity still find that they struggle to use the tools effectively. No matter how great the system is, an email organization tool won't do the work for you. No tricks or tips for becoming better at budgeting will think for you. The main issue for people who have a hard time with productivity is not an inability to learn new systems, but a lack of discipline.

The New Muscle

You can think of self-discipline as a new muscle that you haven't worked out before. At first, it's going to be a little tough, but it will get stronger the more you use it. Building your self-discipline from the point of view of productivity is being able to just do what you need to do. Depending on the field it pertains to, self-discipline can mean a variety of different things. If you're a musician, it can mean picking up your guitar every afternoon, even when you'd rather watch TV. If you're dedicated to learning a language, it means dedicating time each day to practicing.

Creating Results

But the most very helpful definition you can use for self-discipline is a tool to create results in your life. Everyone has ideas, but it's only the people who can get themselves to act that get any good results from them. Coming up with a system for organizing or processing email won't matter if you don't actually implement the new system when you have a chance.

Tips for Disciplined Productivity

But this knowledge is only the first step. Knowing something does not mean you will be productive. Only implementation can guarantee results. As stated, anyone can have a concept in their head, but it's only the people who know how to make themselves act on their ideas that will enjoy the success we all look up to and crave. Here are some tips for getting there.

1. Start Out Small

If you've never been able to bring about small ideas in your life, then it's going to be hard to make something huge happen immediately. Sure, it may work for someone every once in a while to attack a momentous goal and succeed at it right away, but for the rest of us, starting out small is going to be the best course of action. Let's return to the comparison of being disciplined to using a new muscle.

If you've never worked out your arms before, do you think you'd be able to lift an extremely heavy item?

No. And you won't be able to build a successful business or valuable, worthwhile habit overnight either. Here are some ideas for small changes you can begin implanting today:

- **Drinking More Water:** If you have a goal of losing weight, for example, it won't happen overnight. You are going to have junk food cravings for a while. But you can start with a small change like replacing your soda with lemon water or drinking your coffee without sugar. This can make a bigger difference in your weight than you realize.

- **Making Small Agreements:** If you're struggling with productivity or self-discipline, another good place to start is by making small appointments that you must stick to no matter

what happens. This can be calling your mom
every week, or something related to your
business.

- **Unplug and Recharge:** More and more,
  people are starting to realize the benefit of
  turning off their computers and phones to
  allow their minds to rest. This small change can
  pave the way for a lot more productivity
  because you'll get the break you need. Try
  starting with just an hour of being phone-free
  per day, then work your way up.

Now, these changes may seem small or insignificant
on their own, but they will add up to huge changes
over time. And more importantly, you will learn that
you have it in you to change any time you want to.
With these small changes, your sense of self-discipline

will slowly rise. Before you know it, you'll be tackling far bigger changes and feeling like a brand-new person!

2. Check Your Expectations

It would be a mistake to expect a weak muscle to be as strong as a muscle you're accustomed to using on a regular basis, and this also applies to your self-discipline muscle. Make sure that you aren't giving yourself unrealistic expectations or this will be much harder than it has to be.

3. Stay Accountable

When an individual has atrophied muscles and can no longer use them, they have to take intense therapy to rebuild strength. They must start out small and gradually increase the load until their muscles work again. This can also happen to your self-discipline, so you have to find a way to stay accountable. Whether this means signing up for a group or finding a partner who you can check in with, accountability is going to keep you on the right track towards your goals and keep you disciplined.

Try finding a person who is encouraging and helpful, who will be present in your daily life and wants to aid you in your goals. If you're trying to form a specific habit for professional reasons, then it can be a work colleague. But habits that have to do with your home life might be a little more complicated. If your goal is to quit smoking, for example, you may need a friend or relative to help you stay accountable. It's even better if this individual has the same goal as you, so you can lean on each other. If you don't know anyone in your life, check out groups online for support.

4. Give Yourself Challenges

For most people, routine can be the biggest enemy of success. This leads to sitting on the couch night after night or spending way too much time scrolling Facebook instead of pursuing worthwhile activities. But getting stuck in a rut like this will ensure that nothing new or exciting ever happens to us. And that's a serious issue. Contrary to popular belief, passion and enthusiasm are the byproducts of taking action, not the reasons for it.

- **Try New Things:** Figuring out what you care most about in life is going to take some time. And until you know, you'll probably be a pro at finding countless excuses for not pursuing more worthwhile activities. The fact is that no one knows how they will feel about something unless they try.

- **If TV Disappeared:** Ask yourself what you would spend your days doing if the television and Facebook suddenly disappeared and you had to leave your house each day to do something. Would you go back to school? Learn how to salsa dance? Take up snowboarding? It's time to stop putting off these activities and take action now.

Chapter 4: Meditation and Focus in Self-Discipline

The average person thinks that meditation is a mystical or difficult activity, but the truth is that it's very simple. Meditation can improve your self-discipline and focus in amazing ways. There are countless techniques for meditation, but it's best to start out with something simple at first. No one is good at meditation when they start out, but that's the point of practicing. You will soon learn as you continue practicing that you can stay with an activity, even if it seems hard.

Simple Beginner Meditation

You don't have to be a Buddhist to meditate. You can even start getting into the swing of it now. Throughout the day, start reminding yourself to focus on your breath and clear your mind. You can even set reminders on your phone. Go as long as you can focus on your breath and noticing every thought that comes up. Once you've done this for a few days, it's time to move onto sitting meditation:

1. **Sit Down:** The first step is to simply sit down. Some are flexible enough to sit cross-legged on the floor on a cushion comfortably, but most people will need to use a chair. If sitting in a chair with a straight back is uncomfortable for you, you can lie down, but try not to fall asleep.

2. **Keep Your Eyes Closed:** Now, gently close your eyes and keep them shut for the duration of this practice. Start breathing normally, but maybe a little deeper than you usually would. Try to breathe through the belly, allowing your abdomen to rise and fall, instead of through the

chest.

3. **Start with 2 Minutes:** When you first begin this practice, start with setting your alarm for only 2 minutes. This may sound like a pointless amount of time, but it's important to slowly ease into this. As you get comfortable with these 2-minute intervals, you can begin working your way up to longer periods.

Most people will get frustrated when they learn to meditate because they will find that their mind is extremely loud and active, trying to pull them away from sitting calmly. This is something you should expect and plan for, because it happens to everyone. This is normal and don't let it upset you. Just stay with it and be patient and it will get easier and easier. Soon, you may even find yourself looking forward to your meditation sessions when you notice how much calmer and more focused they make you.

There's No Such Thing as "Trying"

When we are "trying" to get something done, we may use limited time as an excuse not to complete anything. Perhaps it's a work project that you're trying to do, but you keep telling yourself that you only have a half hour of free time and that's not enough to get anything substantial done. Under this logic, watching TV or doing chores sounds like the more sensible thing to do. You tell yourself that you are "trying" to do something, when a lot of the time, that's simply not the case. You are either doing something or you aren't.

- **Avoidance:** Many times, trying is our way of choosing avoidance because we're afraid of something. Maybe we're afraid to change, afraid to disappoint our parents, or afraid of judgment from our peers for doing something different. Claiming to ourselves that we are trying is a convenient method for avoiding a commitment while pretending that you have committed. It's an avoidance tactic.

- **Change Your Language:** You must realize that the language of "trying" will make you fall short, because trying is not action. It's procrastination. Pay attention to the words you choose to use and keep in mind that you can either choose to do something or choose not to. Own your decisions. Be honest with yourself about why you choose or don't choose to do something.

- **Admit when You Don't Want to:** Instead of telling yourself that you're trying when you aren't, instead admit that you don't want to do something. This will either help you realize that you can still choose to get the task done, or help you come up with a plan for a better time to do it. Be real with yourself so you can perfect your sense of self-discipline.

Chapter 5: Avoiding Burnout and Overcoming Resistance

The Pareto principle, also known as the 80/20 rule is very effective for better time management. This principle states that 80 percent of your results in life are going to come from 20 percent of the actions you take. This realization will help you change your process of setting and achieving goals. This principle was named after Vilfredo Pareto in the year 1895 when he noticed there were about 20 percent of people who succeeded, while the rest fell into the bottom 80 percent.

He soon realized that almost all activity in economics also adhered to this pattern. 20 percent of people controlled 80 percent of wealth in Italy then. And this principle can be applied to many different situations for us today. You can use this to prioritize your days and tasks and become more productive and disciplined with your goals. So how exactly does the principle work? If you make a list of 10 items you need to get done, two items on the list are more important than the remaining 8 items. But the sad truth is that many people put off the top 20 percent of task items that matter the most, focusing instead on the other 8 items that don't matter much and won't bring them real success.

Using the Pareto Principle for Goals

You can use this principle for more effective goal-setting and to enhance your discipline. Follow these simple rules and you will be successfully applying the 80/20 principle and thriving as a result.

- **Make a List:** Begin by writing your 10 most important goals of the moment. Then figure out which one of them you would choose if you had to select the goal that will have the biggest payoff in your current situation. Place a number 1 next to that task. Next, choose the follow-up goal in terms of importance. You will soon realize that once you've completed this exercise that you've identified the 20 percent that will be most worthwhile. Focus on those before the others. Here are some more steps to help you along the way.

- **Tackle the Hardest Goal First:** The world is full of people who look like they're always busy but who hardly get anything done. That's because they are usually busying themselves with tasks that aren't very important, putting off the harder and more important goals. The valuable activities are usually the harder ones, but they will lead to a greater payoff. Just tackle the bigger goals first and the rest of your day will be a breeze. Resist the urge to do the easier tasks first.

- **Keep Your Eyes Ahead:** Although it's good to break your goals into smaller and more manageable tasks, you should have one major goal that keeps you motivated and disciplined to continue. This will be your fuel for the days that you'd rather lie around and be lazy. If your goal is to become the top CEO of your company, print out a photo of a successful businessman that you will look at every day. This can represent your vision of success. If you want to move into your dream home within five years, set your phone background as a picture of a similar house. These tricks will help you keep your major goal in mind at all times, even when the going gets tough.

Tips for Preventing Burnout

Although self-discipline sounds like being tough on yourself, it also involves knowing when to take a break. Without them, you will eventually burn out. Burnout gets in the way of your ability to think clearly and creatively, making you think in more rigid ways. This is what happens when you work overtime every single week and don't make time for relaxation or de-stressing. Here are some tips you can follow to prevent burnout, so you can stay on task with your goals.

Make Time for Creativity

What is your favorite creative activity? It could be singing, painting, or dancing. Whatever it is, make some time for it and don't neglect the enjoyment of the activity because you believe it isn't productive. Even when you can't apply that creative skill to your professional life, this outlet will help you de-stress and recover from your workload, keeping you motivated and engaged.

Get Up Often

If you, like so many other modern-day people, sit at a desk all day, you need to make sure you're standing up and moving around often. Most people stay sitting at their desks even when they're on break, operating under the illusion that the more immersed in their work they are, the better off they'll be. But the truth is that you aren't a machine and you need a break. Our bodies are built to move around, not sit sedentary all day. Try to stand up and stretch or take a quick walk around the office at least once an hour, but even more than that is better if you can.

Don't Avoid Others

Support is important for human beings, and more and more of them have no one to confide in about their personal issues, according to research. It's true that the more stressed out or exhausted we fell, the more we want to be alone, oftentimes. But the fact is that that is the last thing you should do in that situation. Make time for social interaction, even when you don't feel like it. You will be surprised at how big of a difference it makes in how you feel.

Kill the People-Pleaser

But just as important as it is to make time for social interaction with other people, it's equally crucial to make sure we're listening to our own inner guidance instead of others when it matters the most. Many of us say "yes" to people at work or in our personal lives just because it's easier to avoid confrontation, even when we're exhausted and need some time to unwind alone. Notice when you do this and try to get rid of the habit of being a people-pleaser.

Be Solution-Oriented

We already dedicated a section in the book to the importance of positivity, and this is a somewhat related point. Positivity makes you more creative and resilient, enabling you to think in terms of solutions instead of avoidance. The more you tune into positivity when you're on the brink of burning out, the more you will learn how to relax and recognize when you need a break. If your main goal is being productive at work, it pays to remind yourself that you won't be very successful if you keep going until your positivity (and as a result, your creativity and innovative thinking) has completely run out. Take the time to rest and recharge your batteries.

Overcoming Resistance

People are afraid of change. We are creatures of habit and like to stay in our familiar routines and bubbles without being disturbed. In fact, this is so true that people often dislike when *others* change too, even if it has nothing to do with them. Do you struggle with sticking by your heart's desires because you're afraid of what others will say? The truth is that people like stability and homeostasis, and they want you to remain predictable. But is that a reason to throw away your values and settle for a life you don't really want?

When you change in real ways, it will force the people around you to change too because they'll have to find new ways to respond to your shifts. A lot of people don't like this and will resist it. They might try to talk you out of a new job or a new look and won't be interested in hearing your logical reasoning behind your choice. How can you handle these reactions, both from other people and yourself? Should you give up on changing and stay the same old predictable you? Absolutely not! Here are some preparations you can make to handle resistance better.

1. Know Your Reasons

When your mind (or mother) begins to give you reasons why you shouldn't try something new, have your main motivation in mind. Don't allow this truth to waver at all and keep your mind on it no matter what happens. Be ready to defend yourself, if necessary, but don't go picking a fight. When you know exactly why you're doing something, words to the contrary have no bearing on you. If you are confident in your choices, the opinions of others (or of your own insecure side) won't be able to change your mind.

2. Have a Comeback Ready

Plan out what you will say if someone tries to talk you out of something you've already decided on. This comeback could be funny, logical, or whatever feels right to you. Imagine that you're about to make a career change and pursue the job you really want, but that you're leaving your old career behind and want to tell your parents about it. Think of what the likeliest response will be to your news, ("But you've had that job for 10 years, it would be foolish to quit now!") and prepare what you will say ahead of time. Make it clear that you aren't looking to be talked out of your choice.

3. Make New Friends Who Get it

It can be hard to follow a specific path if you aren't surrounded by people who understand it. If you don't have any friends who can support your new goal, it may be time to seek out some new ones. Join a club that revolves around your interest, or even an internet forum where you can discuss it. Support is crucial. Instead of seeking out encouraging words from the people who don't approve of your new way of acting, save your updates for people who do.

4. Share Your Progress (When Asked)

Odds are, when you begin to show that sense of satisfaction and happiness from your new changes, the people in your life will want some of what you're having. If you can tell that someone wants more information on how you made your change, be there to offer insight and tips. Don't preach to them about it, but answer questions if they ask. Change doesn't happen overnight, but you can be a good resource for someone if they are interested in taking a similar path or pursuing their own goal.

5. Be Tough

There are going to be instances where this new path you've chosen feels lonely and difficult. But this has to be your motivation to continue. When you push through these hard times, you have a chance to make real, lasting changes. This is what real self-discipline is all about; staying on your path even when it isn't easy. It's what separates the amazing achievers from the average Joes. Make a list of all the reasons why you are going after whatever your specific goal is. Any time you're struggling, review the list so you can remind yourself why you're doing what you're doing.

6. Remember That It's a Process

Don't ever forget that success is not just a single step, but an ongoing process. As soon as you achieve what you wanted more than anything in one area, there will be something else worth going after before you know it. Success is a long, varied path that you must be truly dedicated to in order to succeed.

Now you have all the tools you need to succeed in life. If you stick to the steps in this book, you will experience a total, radical shift in your self-discipline. With this information, you can become as fit as you want, find a new career, or build a beautiful relationship with your partner. You can apply these basic principles to your life no matter what your goal is.

Chapter 6 Final Thoughts

Thanks for picking up *Self-Discipline and Mental Toughness: A Guide to Developing Your Grit and Increasing Your Productivity*. I hope that this book gave you the inspiration you need to become a more self-disciplined individual and as a result, achieve your deepest dreams in life.

Life is full of problems and challenges along the path to achievement and success. But to get past these, you must be persistent, persevere, and develop a strong identity of self-discipline. This skill will give you healthy self-esteem, confidence in all you do, and satisfaction and general life happiness, as well. If you ignore or neglect to develop self-discipline, on the other hand, you could be looking at loss, failures, bad relationships, and low self-worth.

Whether your goal is to overcome a negative habit, improve your study habits, exercise more often, or rise to the top in your professional field, you need this skill. There are plenty of books out there on the market about self-discipline, so thank you for choosing this one. If you found it helpful, please take the time to leave it a review on Amazon! Thanks again and good luck out there.

The following eBook is reproduced below with the goal of providing information that is as accurate and as reliable as possible. Regardless, purchasing this eBook can be seen as consent to the fact that both the publisher and the author of this book are in no way experts on the topics discussed within, and that any recommendations or suggestions made herein are for entertainment purposes only. Professionals should be consulted as needed before undertaking any of the action endorsed herein.

This declaration is deemed fair and valid by both the American Bar Association and the Committee of Publishers Association and is legally binding throughout the United States.

Furthermore, the transmission, duplication or

reproduction of any of the following work, including

precise information, will be considered an illegal act,

irrespective whether it is done electronically or in

print. The legality extends to creating a secondary or

tertiary copy of the work or a recorded copy and is

only allowed with express written consent of the

Publisher. All additional rights are reserved.

The information in the following pages is broadly

considered to be a truthful and accurate account of

facts, and as such any inattention, use or misuse of the

information in question by the reader will render any

resulting actions solely under their purview. There are

no scenarios in which the publisher or the original

author of this work can be in any fashion deemed

liable for any hardship or damages that may befall them after undertaking information described herein.

Additionally, the information found on the following pages is intended for informational purposes only and should thus be considered, universal. As befitting its nature, the information presented is without assurance regarding its continued validity or interim quality. Trademarks that mentioned are done without written consent and can in no way be considered an endorsement from the trademark holder.

Description

In *Self-Discipline and Mental Toughness: A Guide to Developing Your Grit and Increasing Your Productivity,* you will learn:

- **Motivation vs. Discipline:** Most of us seek motivation, but what exactly is this quality? Although it can be a useful tool or mindset for achieving greatness, it's not always as reliable as you might think. Chapter one will tell you what type of motivation is most reliable and also how self-discipline can, in many cases, be superior to simple motivation.

- **Finding Your Purpose:** What do you want to be remembered for when you die? What is your deepest purpose in life? These are tough questions for most of us. Chapter two will walk you through these questions, and more, so you can get to the root of your values and goals and live a more meaningful life.

- **How to Handle Failure:** Did you know that failure can be a great advantage on the path to success? It's all in how you approach it mentally. In chapter three, and throughout the rest of the book, we will illustrate how and why this is the case, so you can reframe your perspective on failure and mistakes.

- **Meditation and Focus:** If you spend a fair amount of time online, you may already know about all of the great health benefits of meditation. In chapter four, we will cover how meditation can improve your focus and self-discipline, as well as give you specific instructions for how to start meditating today.

- **Avoiding Burnout:** Burnout is what happens when you don't give yourself a break and you work too hard. There are tips and techniques for avoiding this unfortunate state, which we will cover in chapter five. In this chapter, we will also go over how to overcome resistance to change, both in others and yourself.

As you can see, this book is full of valuable tips that can bring serious changes to your life. If you're ready to stop making excuses and procrastinating, it's about time you learned how to develop self-discipline. This guide will help you do that.